AMANDA

PARADISE

AMANDA PARADISE

RESURRECT EXTINCT VIBRATION

by CAConrad

WAVE BOOKS / SEATTLE AND NEW YORK

Published by Wave Books

www.wavepoetry.com

Copyright © 2021 by CAConrad

All rights reserved

Wave Books titles are distributed to the trade by

Consortium Book Sales and Distribution

Phone: 800-283-3572 / SAN 631-760X

Library of Congress Cataloging-in-Publication Data

Names: Conrad, C. A., author.

Title: Amanda paradise : resurrect extinct vibration / by CAConrad.

Description: First edition. | Seattle : Wave Books, [2021]

Identifiers: LCCN 2021009918 | ISBN 9781950268436 (hardcover) | ISBN
9781950268429 (paperback)

Subjects: LCGFT: Poetry.

Classification: LCC PS3603.O555 A82 2021 | DDC 811/.6—dc23

LC record available at https://lccn.loc.gov/2021009918

Designed by CAConrad

Printed in the United States of America

9 8 7 6 5 4 3 2 1

First Edition

Wave Books 094

for the abandoned
storming the dream

AMANDA

PARADISE

GOLDEN IN THE MORNING CRANE OUR NECKS

in a past life I was
a little fish who
cleaned the
shells of
turtles
a dream
helped me
remember their
deep voice of thanks
many nights I heard sharks waiting
for the tide to draw me near
when the calendar runs out
it feels lucky another awaits
all I have ever wanted was to
forge the English language into
a spear and drive it into my heart
between leaping and being shoved
no lonelier place to put my faith for the
swinging motion inside the dance we share
don the extraordinary suit for this ordinary day
take our time studying trees to imagine the
nests we would build if we were birds
I ask all
you talented
people spending
many creative hours
perfecting killer drones
guns and bombs to please
know we are waiting for
you on the other side
of art in the No
Kill Zone

I

ON ALL FOURS I AM A SEAT FOR THE WIND

most of my family's
international travel
is being sent to war
if we judge love we
can kill off anything
dragged by our hair
across the days until
they make their way
inside our dreams where we get to evict them
I want to thank the one who invented knocking on the door
but no one remembers their name to tattoo across my knuckles
I asked an archaeologist about first time she stuck a shovel in the ground
her answer had same restorative powers as the gravedigger's
when we die we can no longer wipe the muck off
just lie there becoming shit of the world
eat a chip of your own dried blood
join me in the cannibal sunshine
fully persuaded by the
world through song
each morning a blue
jay screams at edge
of the clear-cut forest
I scream with her at
the bleeding stumps
scream inside something
borrowed like ocean like skin
I want to see before I die a
mink wearing a human scarf
skin from a handsome
hairy leg
MEOW

ACCLIMATING TO DISCOMFORT OF THE SYSTEM BREAKING BENEATH US

I do not take any
calls except from
the century we are in
when there is no bible in my hotel room
it makes me sad to have no place to put
my filthy poems for future guests
it is important to let them know
everyone should burn with abandon as soon as the heat is available
be a self-styled alarm clock no one can shut off
be the storm Love places in someone's home
are you sure we can handle this
because I am absolutely certain
c'mon wind knock us around
we are a tide that cures ills
look at us in the mirror
as soon as the invented language enters
us something else will vibrate in our skin
opening door with teeth of the future to
the place where we let the freer feeling go
when you told me you had been looking for me
we pressed through every
invisible barrier between us
I watched you gently let the gods
know you are ready to win the lottery
there were people from the
19th century alive in my
lifetime many years ago
I met some of them
they are all gone now
as we hold on to
the side of one
another howling down
the velocity of seconds

900 CHOCOLATE HEARTS A MINUTE AT THE CANDY FACTORY

estimate number of
near-misses after
interrupting the
angel prying your
father's jaws apart
fashioned on tip of a fork
car horn at door to the birth canal
living section of dawn cooking inside the poet
today is the day we reject this vexing sell-by-date worry
no guarantee we will cohere in our broken patch of garden
when you look at me you see
mostly water who will
one day hasten to
join a cloud
a thing I know for
certain is to cook
companionship into
food to taste and
become fellowship
eat a leaf with a hole
to share nourishment
with a future butterfly
you believe in sharing
at least you used to
I know you want
to shock me with
reports of enjoying
gloryholes and I can
act shocked to amuse
you yet I wonder if you
ever look up to the wall
thinking it will be his eyes

AUGURIES CAST ASIDE

to enter the sky with our bodies
the principal concern for
inventing airplanes
no one taught me this
any more than they taught me
to say good morning to my hippocampus
but I do because I love my hippocampus
I was in a band one summer
we never could harmonize
we smiled and kept playing
we loved our united disunity
a frantic enraptured focus
chewing its way out
how awkward the
archer after
shooting
his arrow
remembering
first time getting
into bed just
for sex
they say
I'm old now
ask my advice
all I have to offer is
make as many mistakes as
you can handle but make them
as soon as possible and please do
not waste time following each other
from opposite sides of the river
when storm blows wig off
my head it simply means
it is time to let the
storm take
its share

ONLY IN STACKING BOOKS CAN THE TREE FEEL ITS WEIGHT AGAIN

I am so fucking sick of nations
and the men who love them
the number of suicides
this afternoon hiding
in bottom of a cup
I feel feral out here
found a man who likes me like that
found a man who lives the way I do
7 years on the road anniversary soon
you only have to destroy
yourself for love until it is normal
which makes love normal
and refuse to live a day without it
an inferno of it
at 16 sleeping with
my mother's boyfriend
I was overwhelmed with it
solids form around you until you
struggle no more beneath it
feel throat open in a word
naming new stars moving across
the ceiling from the disco ball
constellations with stories to
soften hardened hearts
we finish the night
reading poetry out loud
last night Erica Kaufman's
mind-blowing *Post Classic*
poetry and love
sure know how to
hang a Welcome sign out
measure and transmit from
the pink and adorable telemetry
no more waiting between parentheses
we now excel in the ether while holding hands

DEATH WILL SET YOUR DAY RIGHT

pigeon cleaning her wings
perched on brass feather of
General So-and-So's statue
we have each other's
embrace a few
years at most
could be we
engineered this wrong
wobbled into universe fixing
long goals with a toothpick
I am greedy too with time
have given myself to the hem of it
walked on knees for gifts to continue
longing pushed to the back of the barrel
listened to draining wound paddling its waters
hold us upwards Shadow it is by you we are cradled
I am not a masochist I tire quickly from pain
interrogate flyswatter
knife and fork as
accessories to
a crime
how many
times do I forget
I must die?
(((((((((simple (((((((((
as many times
a day I am
not your
humble
fellow
human

BATHE THE DOOR WITH BLOOD OF THE CENTAUR

when orders
for evacuation
come over loudspeakers
the forest is at the center of the predicament
their position keeps changing in the back room
dolling up the F-word with sequins
we know what is coming is the
oldest malediction against gravity
keeping pressure on the wound
writhing against
impressions the
center brought us
a new kind of anvil
dropped without the
slightest apprehension
we later lapse into a season of latent beauty
leveling quiet towns in their sleep
somewhere north of here the beginning of
the Mississippi is a bucket of water
we tilt our
ears from
blankets of
sweat and cum
overhearing birds in
their temples of the trees

FOR THE FERAL SPLENDOR THAT REMAINS
for Kazim Ali

sometimes I strain
to hear one
natural
sound
when gender blurs in a
poem my world sets a
tooth in the gear
if god is in me
when will I ask for
my needs to be met
every god is qualified
it is not such a secret
when I was afraid of the
road I learned to drive
map says name of
your city in ocean
line drawn to it
towing behind
the big party
history of life on
earth might be
interesting to a
visitor one day
chewing parsley and
cilantro together is for
me where forest
meets meadow
in a future life
would we like to
fall in love with the
world as it is with
no recollection
of the beauty
we destroy
today

ALTERED AFTER TOO MANY YEARS UNDER THE MASK

I feel you
judging me for
becoming agoraphobic
in someone else's house
I forget how I learned to stroll through
grocery stores as though there is no crisis
my elbow cannot touch the middle of my back
my fingers though have found every part of me
soon no migration of wild animals will
be unknown to humans we will chart
film record publish archive everything
it gives us something to do while we
annihilate beauty poets shoveling
a quarry that is really an ongoing
crime scene investigation
a study in vomit imitating
vast chronicles of the face
whatever world we can hold
we will never agree our
neglect was worth it
whatever amount of
crazy we can imagine
coming at us double it
I found the perfect
listening chair nothing
but listeners who sit
I am sitting in it now
listening to my friend
the photographer
whose self-portrait
I find reflected
in eyes
of her
every
photo

EMBEDDED SIGNAL TO SHAKE THE DAY

do you have
the strength to
lose this world
earlier today I pushed
a daffodil back in its bulb
don't listen to the impossible
not when they're drowning in snow
everyone wants to share with you the
lines they crossed to get here
all indicators say we have
been target practice for
the gods long enough
in the downpour
on the highway
we get slow
together
for millions
of years the
river flowed
without bridges
dams casinos
one day death
will just click
into every future
with the right quiet we can
listen to the crackling
fire that keeps us
98.6 degrees
Fahrenheit
yes my answer when he
asked if swallowing
semen made him
a cannibal

NO ONE HOLDING IT SHUT

he called me a morbid son
of a bitch and it gave me pause
enjoying a love song written by a
woman who died one day despite
her intimate care for the
world around her
may our levees hold
may our strength return
a meow avowing a roar
there has been no one
since he died who can
be there in my chest
lift me into morning
believe in love again
someone said not to write about
love which is a conversation we can have
after I am finished writing this love poem
holding a fist of wheat in the wind
a day to be as small as possible
following thoughts to their smells or
sit and listen for the archive to waken
the night before moving I woke
then decided to go back to
sleep for one more dream in
the apartment where I loved him
when he was alive
actually and completely
real flesh with fingers pressing
glow-in-the-dark stars and planets
above the bed and turning
to smile and join me
on the pillow

YOU CANNOT RETURN A STRETCHED MIND

human life expectancy is rising
I ask which group they mean
no one knows the answer
my favorite lovers were
men who knew they were dying
they taught me to race to my limits without hesitation
sometimes it takes more death than I can endure to caress life
if you could have seen my face the moment I realized no help was coming
despite every dream of
lovers around the
globe uniting
grateful for our embrace to
hold the sadness different
we are too fragile for the
world we are making
pretending to be tough
a sudden fear of heights over the Atlantic
flock of dead lovers leaving with the geese
transmit psychic code to *go Go GO*
saying AIDS aloud enters
each body uniquely
cells memorize
all abyss survived
please say today
is the day we
accept our
family
as every
neighbor

GLITTER IN MY WOUNDS

first and most important
dream our missing friends forward
burn their reflections into empty chairs
we are less bound by time than the clock maker fears
this morning all I want is to follow where the stone angels point
birdsong lashing me to tears
heterosexuals need to see our suffering
the violent deaths of our friends and lovers
to know glitter on a queer is not to dazzle but to
unsettle the foundation of this murderous culture
defiant weeds smashing up through cement
you think Oscar Wilde was funny
well Darling I think he was busy
distracting straight people
so they would not kill him
if you knew how many times I
have been told *you're not like my*
gay best friend who tells me
jokes and makes me laugh
no I sure as fuck am not
I have no room in my life to
audition for your pansy mascot
you people can't kill me and
think you can kill me again
I met a tree in Amsterdam and
stood barefoot beside it for twenty
minutes then left completely restored
yet another poem not written by a poet
sometimes we need one muscle to
relax so the others follow
my friend Mandy calls after a
long shift at the strip club to say
while standing in line for death I am
fanning my hot pussy with your new book
will you sign it next week my fearless faggot sister

WE VANISH INTO ONE ANOTHER AS NEEDED
for Dara Wier

in the middle of surgery the doctor asks if
we want to make use of the open chest
feed love notes and lucky numbers to
the bird under the ribcage
ask it how to stop
blaming violets for
adapting beneath
mower blades
it is a choice to not
be offended when
your lover says there
is no extra room in his
survivalist bunker
shocked by
spaces between
molecules we
thought were
holding us
together
old ghosts
moving into the
new apartment
my name is
Amanda Paradise
an intestinal
expatriate
the kind of
bitch who yells
HUMANS ARE THE INVASIVE SPECIES
every time they point at a pretty
flower and say it is not
being pretty in the
right place

IMPALED BY SHARP POINTS OF WONDERMENT

he
insisted
I should know
names of extinct species
as though taxonomy ever meant preservation
telling someone who they are
instead of asking is where
extinction gets its start
another window into the
carefully ornamented shadow
you call tails while the
double-headed coin
flies through the air
you say the new
prison means
good paying jobs
for generations
this is where I expect my vomit to land
you start using your therapist as
a weapon against your friends
you pay to be told new
furniture cannot combat
the death of your bedroom
I imagine prison guards not yet born
having lunch inside their parents
study design of the owl's
feathers to study
arms race of
the night

DIVING INTO THE PREMONITION

parents who brought children
to witch burnings
remind me of
parents
where I
grew up
motion of an apple in sunshine
imagine you have
control of the
orchard but
imagination
is all you
control
wolves give birth in late April an
entire species of Tauruses
pups quiver on the green
tendering the open gesture
my body pulled off the road
my spirit takes
me on the American
highways in my sleep
push and push it into
digital mycelium of
the internet
these cells
can never end
the last of the
hand-me-downs
I slept in his shirt for
a year after he died
now I would rather
wrap myself
in leaves

THE ASKING PRICE

when people purchase
the documentary about
me also purchase *Twin
Peaks* and *The X-Files*
it speaks to the
fiction I become
two surfer dudes told us
a pod of orcas were eating
the extra seals in the harbor
extra never felt
so jeopardized
acing the lost-virtue test
rain silenced for just a
second when driving
under the bridge
I have heard your
story before Weed For A
Fortnight That Lasts Four Nights
have you heard about the extra surfer dudes
you were drunk when you
asked me to change the
weather but I did it
bleeding on correct
patch of garden like
my love for you in
this poem which is not
from the planet we imagined
you were beautiful sprawled naked in the back of your truck
you made me forget a line I
wanted to write down
I will see our love in
the missing part of
the poem every
time I read it

ENCIRCLING THIS DAY WITH CENTIPEDE COORDINATION

Dear Eileen have we sunk the shine
the maintenance man at this place
asked if I needed help relaxing tonight
HAHA I told him to throw my door
open whenever he wanted
and HE FUCKING DID IT
when men do as I say
it saves so much time
he prolonged a certain
mediation of reality a
day when my pronoun
choice is uppity cunt
I imagine 9 things
close my eyes until
they are connected
after moving around for
years I knew if I rested to lay
his filthy hand against my chest
little critter under my tires
roadkill changing to armadillos
tell a lie to steal time for this poem
some days there is no problem
and it is terrifying
let's not get used to that
let's stop believing that
my Capricorn horns digging
pits in the earth a surplus of
pits to bury what may
not want to let go
cars feeding crows
coyotes and vultures
he asked if poetry
could possibly fulfill me
but it is the study of everything

CAMISADO

after breaking in
the wolf
calmed
the hens
so he could
take his time with them
twists them open until the right
amount of memory fits into the song
another high price for belonging
poetry is the opposite of escape
but makes this world endurable
how the smallest puddle
reflects the entire sky
a return to every dream
our minds talked us out of
trusting our math of the star
your hand around my shoulder
poet astronaut you know I love you
I have no sense of failure when I am with you
everything matters because everything
hurts someone somewhere as it is mattering
we became all we carried into the mast
migratory patterns given to the love again
a way to end this secrecy of suffering
cut a door in the wolf so we
can retrieve our dead for
a world that matters

ON THE 10TH ANNIVERSARY OF THE DISAPPEARANCE OF
AMERICA'S ANTIWAR MOVEMENT WHILE THE WARS RAGE ON
for Sarah Fox

his fig leaf flutters on the electric
fan to reveal the true gift of this god
a long-stemmed rose with a sad story to hide
America is all about growing that hair back keeping that cock stiff
empire crumbling around world's most obstinate hard-on
a stick with a fur coat limping through the forest
this bus runs on *clean* natural gas
lies from our government and
lies of corporations seem to
      find common ground
      not too much trouble
      when you are one of
      9 tomatoes resting in
      a blender just above the On button
            our planet had herds of triceratopses
            can only imagine their lost sounds
            were they like lions or loons
            our human sounds all day
            in the hospital
            my friend Adam
            asked me to describe
            the 9 cigarettes smoked
            by Bette Davis in *All About Eve*
            gaps in the hero of the moment
            each puff a meditation on betrayal
            held by the indestructible power of 9
            faithless treachery known by many
     Salvador Dalí publicly praising
   Franco's iron fist even after Franco
executed Dalí's former lover
       the great poet of the people
           Federico García Lorca

MEMORIES OF WHY I STOPPED BEING A MAN
for Jason Dodge

it's normal
if your cock
gets hard while
you are shooting
my uncle told me
on my first deer hunt
Pythagoras knew the music
of Jupiter and Mercury
long before NASA
but to begin again
no hero itching
at the door
that never-ending search for weakness in
neighbors siblings coworkers rival football teams
after seeing the open body of muscle and blood
we had horrible ideas about what to do with our lives
imagine how they gathered around the first
cannon ever fired sweaty excited rock hard
before he died Kalashnikov confessed
to suffering unbearable nightmares
surrender your nouns to my verbs
he said he said he said he said
in a game of Russian roulette
I won a pair of glasses
that can see the wind
I walk around town each night watching the
slightest breeze approach dry leaves like a premonition
after a million years of dreaming
the solution is still the same
hold me to your bruised song
until it warms me right

when I learned male lions kill and
eat another male's cubs I was
desperate to get my sister
away from our horny
violent stepfather
where were you
Amanda Paradise
when I was 10 she was 6
lean back in chair fall all over it
believing milk comes from clouds
insert straw and suck the word *choice* dry
vacuum cleaners and lawn mowers our
demoralized efforts to contain chaos
wear a touch of mask this evening
tell the children when US poets pay
their taxes homes of poets in the
Middle East burn to the ground
we lift higher and stronger on the
stock market's wingspan of annihilation
imagination of mouse flying by in owl's talons
torn from secure location stampede in the chest
in a trance to recall first time I saw the sun as a child
Gumby almost dies on the moon in the first episode
how were we supposed to fucking feel
I remember panic and confusion in
kindergarten when our teacher was
afraid the 7 dwarves did terrible
things to her as she slept in the
unwritten parts of the book
who are these people and why
did our parents leave us with them

MURDER IS AGAINST A RULE SOMEWHERE THAT IS NOT AMERICA
for Raquel Salas Rivera

harvesting the heads
of our nation's enemies
is what our family does
we must not deny it
taken to the
real world
blindfolded
sentenced before we knew it
I will make you my recipe of tofu cream stuffed
into chocolate with rose petals if you eat it while
talking about truth of suffering with me
our grandfathers and their brothers
killed people in Germany and Japan our
uncles killed people in Korea and Vietnam
today our cousins are killing real live human
bodies in Iraq and Afghanistan
a custom handed down from
crimes of our ancestors
while we put delicious
things in our mouths
how much more
advice will we take
from our false gods
how dare you demand
my success in a nation failing
anything and anyone who is not an agent of war
America honors its soldiers like every empire
rewards its most violent unquestioning citizens
the higher the kill-count the higher the praise
you could become senator of Arizona
how to STOP Americans saying
Vietnam was a war in our foot-
race to Babylon screaming
backwards in the calendar
disturbing Hollywood films
turning Vietnamese people into a
blur of bullets behind every white
hero with cool soundtrack

!! !
for Anne Boyer

I had a boyfriend who
used to bore me with his
guilt for his Faustian bargain
I said *of course you hate yourself*
you sell health insurance
only to find out he never
sold health insurance he
was a claims denier
Devil whatever the fuck
you call someone who
tells someone to die of
cancer because it is not
covered under their plan
I wanted to vomit back the
time I spent with him and
write my poems in peace
I have nothing but exclamation points
for this world some days
one for shock
one for disgust
the third enters into revolution
the awful part about ascension is
something only angels need fear
the first time I heard
politicians say their
feuds must cease before
the holiday shopping season
I understood
someone else was in charge
and theater is never more
revolting as when it
admits the stage

I am the
wagon wishing
you would find me
a maple left uncut
the rock that smashes nothing
seeking a god who speaks to
memories of life before
the heart's affliction
your cum tastes like
hand sanitizer what
have you been up to
when too many die
we deceive despair with love
sex with a man at a funeral
destroying death in his car
a holy perforation for a ghost
for best wish catch apple as it falls
eat seeds and worm to seal your destiny
everyone puts what they've got into the wheel
driving across America
raw imagination faster
than spirits keep up
I cannot remember
the last day a digital
watch was the only
digital object in my life
the first heart transplant
was the last day everyone
alive had hearts we were born with
something to get used to
I was only one year old
but do not remember
anyone objecting to
someone keeping their
strength with someone else's muscle

for years after
 friends died of
  AIDS they still
   danced with me in my dreams
    did survivors of the bubonic plague
    dance with their dead
     who will dance
     with whom
     in a year
     let's
     keep
    safe
   dance
  together
IN PERSON

it was over half my life ago
since I told this many friends
    I hope we all survive
    we did not that time
    but I say it again
    I hope we
    all survive
    I hope we
    all survive

7 years on the road
I am a stray cat now
but only when I am
not writing poems
I slept in my car in Walmart
parking lots across America
not one night
goes by lately
without thinking
of the many people
entire families I met
living in cars with signs
in their windshields
WE NEED DIAPERS
WE NEED FOOD

if we are to dream anything
during this plague
let us please
consider
the things
we do not want
to return to normal

the virus has
  infiltrated every
    part of the United States
      poor people still have to take
        a bus for miles to reach groceries
        empty hotel rooms and casinos
        surround homeless people
        sleeping together
        in a parking lot
        in Las Vegas
       rich men
      making
     state
    governors
   bid and compete
  for lifesaving equipment
while doctors and nurses risk everything they have
who are these men show us their goddamned faces
      the president refuses to call off his ICE militia
      prisoners on hunger strike to prove
      their bodies have limits and needs
        someone on the news just called
          the virus dangerous
            as though this
            violent empire
            was ever safe

some words
cook inside
the mouth
a president's public
disdain for democracy
OUR
connection they
are trying to *(but*
we must never
let them) sever
dance out of
position with me
to the tune of
the spiritual
debt of the
United States
we will not
wait for
them
to say what is next
we belong to another gate

we are 2nd-plague sisters
with daily breath rituals
bridge of breath
for a world of
failing lungs
remember the ones we want to see again
remember them in the deepest breath
web and light
positioned
just right
spider walks
across the
rising sun

the government says to
  practice social distancing
   as though that had
    not been their
   message all
along

it
takes
bodies
to make
this world
there are
no dreams
without us
standing in
the middle
of what we
imagine
for 90 days on the phone
he tells me
it hurts
to not
hold
me
necessity of
love and poetry
incontrovertible

every man in the
UFO documentary is
sexy except the one who does not believe
a stingy imagination is unsexy
possibly the unsexiest
okay
I will
sing
out
the
window
with you
if we promise
to do it the rest of our lives

my best ideas come with
an ear resting on his chest
a holding pattern of the dove
feel our shared thought
thicken the path
it is good to take
it easy on days
when we
remember
we are going
to die
we win everything
for remembering
we are poets

names of water and wind taper
until they resemble everything
eyes closed face tilted into rain
here is the voice to
never let us close accounts
some days I can only
watch movies old
enough every
actor is
dead
this is not morbid
it is the exquisite
transitory chewed upon
reach down pull out
everything we were
told not to touch
gears of the mountain
inside a sleeping bear

my friend
Rex told me
when he was
dying of AIDS
promise me every day of 1993
will be the best day with or without me
27 years later
the promise
still kept

my first meal after his death
a decision to persist without him
please do not attempt to command
the common winds
language shows where we stand
it can reveal how we
care about who is
listening and
how or if we
are listening
we cannot even
be sick together
wishing karma meant
foes against the wall
mr president there is only one
body on the planet whose
gender you get to identify
after that it is none
of your business

in the 1980s
I felt my tonsils
900 times a day
inflicted by
compulsion's
mechanism
until I surrendered
my control to
the ancient
technology
of poetry

New Orleans
travel guide
on table
the news today
is dire down there
a very naked request
to any gods goddesses
angels demons or
whatever devil
can help make
this April not be
the cruelest month

pointing at the
ground and holding it
a new purple on my toes
dirt under feet please guide our course
old man says I look like a freak but
internal magic cannot be contained
in order to live fire
needs to destroy
water can exist
as a calm surf
until it rises up a tsunami
is the
greater impact
to live as fire
or water

43

did someone
come in this
store who has it
does everyone
working here
have
it

singing
got into
everything
until finally
my mind
could not
rob me of
the day

the cat
leaves a
little heat
in the sofa
where I
rest my
hand
what world between
warmth and fever
planet and star

robin sets my ear
kettle sets it
refrigerator engine
the cat's engine
footsteps and
wind can
set it
my lover on the phone
inhale with my
ear set before
the exhale

color of ceiling is
color inside my head
don't stay away too long
I whisper to
myself while
falling asleep
questionnaire
in my fist asking
1- *Number of attempts to walk to the life you desire*
2- *How to keep walking when your mind says Turn Back*

getting used to
hot engine smelling
like celery
when we
develop
our psychic abilities
we prepare to have no
            more hiding places
        our individual vibrations
      merging with the collective
      3rd dimension by day
      awaken to 4th
      by night
      a pounding in the ground
      travels up the spine
      relinquish fear of
      astral travel let's
        push out to give
        the nail a twist
      let's go
      let's go

in a
trance
to recall
first time
I saw the
sun as a
child
I landed on
memory of
first time
mixing
blue
and
red
to make purple
laughing it was
just too amazing
magic lives inside
this

I put my
face in a
small room
called a
scuba
mask
I have carried my room
through larger ones
what did I think
I would see as
everything
imploded
after he
died I tried
to hold him
vibrating in
the middle
of a poem
everyone is always
explaining how
different
being alone
and lonely
but the next
conversation
is how we
have no
choice
but to
die

M   drew
his   face
the day
he was
diagnosed
HIV positive
and kept drawing
as his face changed
they were sublime
like Munch's self
portrait with
Spanish flu
he called on
his deathbed
at his parents'
home to say his
father was in the
backyard burning
the stack of drawings
I wanted to make him stop
please don't he said
it's his last chance to
deny me how can
I deny him that

do you remember
feeling safer before they
said they were going to
make us safe
Hollywood was
eager to control
our imaginations
during the plague
a long bend in
the demon field
persuading us
a black eye
is a story
everyone
wants

a pause
in the
heartbeat
of empire
or never going back
to paying for wars
we pretend are
not happening

                    the governor
                 opened the parks
               and golf courses
            because it would
         not look good to
         open just the
   golf courses
   are they wearing masks at the country club?
   is someone spraying the balls with alcohol?
   are there funny little jokes exchanged
   about social distancing?
   clink-clink the world
   burns burns burns
   burns burns
   burns

Economic Casualties
Ailing Corporations
things reporters say in the USA
Money and its
Masters
dominate
the language
first evidence
of power we
continue to
allow them

Own Your Pussy in the Dark
was the name of a play I lost
with a box of stolen journals
the main character based
on my friend Adam a
street hustler who
died of AIDS
I miss my friend
I can still see the one
typescript in the box
Adam is my Virgil who
guides me to the 18th floor
to leap off the balcony
then climb back up
not a single scratch
to leap again
and leap again
there is a lot of
resurrection and a
revirginizer machine
and a scene where we tie
pinecones to our heads to
honor the swollen pineal gland
of the goddess but that is
all I remember about
Own Your Pussy
in the Dark

we're always
putting words
in the cat's mouth
reading Eileen Myles
poems with pussycat pizzazz
one day for one moment
I could hear exactly
what she thought
I have never seen a
human choke to death
I must keep staring to
not miss my chance
I was shocked I put
the chips down
she yawned
looked away

pastor says the virus is a
punishment for gay rights
my email thanked him
for reminding me
how powerful
we queers are
wielding plagues
with style and grace
Dear Reverend your violent
ignorance is the virus
I point my finger at
you and say aloud
Go Get Him Demon

last spring
I counted 27
dead raccoons
in one day along
the highway killed
while looking for
love little hands
reaching out
over and
over
if you do not think there
is something positive
about this virus
we are all
hiding
from
think
of the
animals

it has
been
so long
you are a
squirrel
someone
used to feed
waiting on a bench

plugging back
of a robin's song
with revving engines
we rest our heads to
acquire revelations
early scientists said
birdsongs were
pleasant but
meaningless
because no one
bothered to ask the
witches strapped to burning stakes
how dare we talk
about Mars as an
option without
giving everything
we have to saving Earth

neither the virus nor
the tornado can
stop the other from racing across the country
there is a tree in Kansas
I hope to see again

I was born
in Kansas but
the first time we heard
a siren in Pennsylvania my
mother screamed *TORNADO*
my 5-year-old feet following her
to the basement
while everyone
upstairs laughed

in this poem
the words I give
you will run out
there is
nothing
I can do
about it
from the
moment I fell in love
with making the letter *g* as a child
I foresaw the peripheries making
g as a conjuring *g g g* curve and
return *g g g* all I wanted for Christmas
was an X-ray of my hand making *g g g*
pleasure in forms united in a life
I choose to love no matter what

after inventing the chair
we built a home around it
memory of splinters from
another part of the tree
every time we open
the door we require
our imaginations to
withstand what we meet
generations later
traveling over
glinting edge of the
skyscraper we finally
appreciate true dearth

my grandmother Pearl said
throw your wallet away the
moment you lose your job
there were many excuses for
losing jobs where I grew up
she was the only
person in my family
in the 1980s who asked
about my dying
lovers and
friends
she said to me after
a week with 3 funerals
there was a beginning to this pain
now you know the middle but
the end too must show itself
when you survive this
love will destroy
all doubt

in a trance
to recall first time
I saw the sun as a child
I made it to 9 when my
aunt Dolly Conrad came
back from vacation as uncle David
returning to the coffin factory he was
not allowed to use the
men's room or women's
they gave him a hole in
the janitor's closet floor
I loved him my queer
hero until he went to
jail for beating
his girlfriend
my first time
hating someone
I once loved

we had much
to leave behind
in order to follow
the river to the sea
my grandfather said
always remember you come
from people who wash after work
        migration can
        change a family
        some die before the end
        others born along the way
                I know my
                poems by
                their shapes
                and have felt
                their edges in
                my dreams the
                side of a poem
                rubbed against
                my cheek like a
                bone comb or
                a lover's toe

my cousin
got jumpy
working at the
slaughterhouse
he could not locate
his strength in the dark
stopping the hearts of
animals for pleasure
some disguise as
survival we now
need to protect
these workers
PLEASE stop
eating flesh
PLEASE let
the blood
stay home

in
my
vegan
dream
birth of the
Goddess Cow who
cannot be fucked with She
who bends every meat blade
every cleaver every bullet deflected
and if you try to make hamburger or
barbecue out of Her family She
puts a hoof
in your
chest
to
push the light out

last year in a
grocery store
in Indiana I met
a family with a
doomsday bunker
the daughter is also a poet
poet like a rock I said
you mean unmovable?
yes until it is time to
smash the empire
her smile electrified
a future poetry
I am excited
to live
to see

I find some in the moth's flight
there is a little in the moon
more than a little in my man
a flower recently gave me enough room to
   accommodate my old friends Chaos and Death
      18-day conversation through a magnifying glass
         a tulip to challenge any artist
            an edifying
            short-lived
            fellowship
             symmetry
            harmony
           rethink
          recode
         engine
         flow

cultivating
interior
life
sounds nice
a rock needed to
float out of my body
it seemed to know the way
the password
is *Gravity*
no need to whisper

tongue turns
lifts holds for
extended vowel
all is pitch-perfect
everyone
loved the speech
no one thanks
the tongue
stagehands
our secret
champions

I love sitting on a bench suddenly when
problems in a poem are clear
I look up 3 hours later
my favorite hours
on this planet
but dare to
look back
and the
game
starts
over

if I could
I would
breast
feed
you
I say
each
morning
after her
first meow

sometimes
crickets allow
us to study their
musical instruments
from palm of our hand
serenade the mythology
crawling under our skin
    codes of spring
    have changed
    their request
    please stop
    holding
      the cloud
      of smoke inside
        the crematorium

the governor set a curfew for 9 pm
helicopters never felt more
urgent passing overhead
the pulse the pulse
the pulse of
blades felt
long after
long after
feel it now
this moment
breath of tree
blooming at window
innnnn   ouuuuuuut   innnnn
ouuuuuuut   innnnn   ouuuuuuut

woke to
@USABrewster
telling me on Twitter
gays deserve to die of AIDS
I told him
Heterosexual Violence is what
I say instead of Homophobia

the
first
time
you
got
high
in
the
morning and stayed there
because you fear the cost of caring
because you get sick when you
hear about war refugees
because you cannot
learn how to undo
yourself to hold
a job and have
friends
but if
we
can
make
a world
we all want
to live in
let's get
building

I have never
sent my sperm
on the journey they
thought they were taking
a short inquisitive tremble
exploring how strange
our human system
hair crawling out
of skulls
enjoying
nature shows
as alligators eat a
grieving monkey's child
snuff films for family time
I was raised to signal through
a set of well-developed
antisocial behaviors
I have witnessed how
much an astronomer's
imagination is set off
Earth and learned
to bring him back
with the proper kiss
attesting to the true
value in the tremors
between us

my boyfriend
calls from
a truck
stop in
Iowa
I can hear the man behind
the counter
is wearing
a mask

HEAVE AWAY MY
JOHNNY
HEAVE
AWAY
when Ray
Bradbury wrote the
screenplay to
Moby Dick
did he sink into his bath
overhearing echoes
from the vast
rooms of
Neptune

no
I do
not
want
to watch
a fucking
pre-plague
reality show
glorifying real
estate the screen
has a THUMBS UP
or SMILEY FACE option that's it
and the omission
of my disgust

US-America
just broke the
record for gun sales
the record we broke
was our own

ready to drop
the certainties
we agree to live as
if there is a set of
spoons we can
stir life with
last year US citizens bought
18,000 tons of bullets for
our undeclared civil war
hiding strength
behind killing
because we are
too weak to find
real solutions
bullets put an
end to the
imagination

we
become
another
kind of bully
for witnessing
without helping
the we in the
leaning tower
of the mind
the oblivious
can only be
interesting
to someone
paying attention
and so
he thought
it best to explain
his misogynistic
joke after she
said *fuck off*

fuck every last
dream of empire
left in middle
of the ocean
with no way
out but through
the bellies of fish
poetry of graffiti
artist reminding
every commuter
CAPITALISM KILLS

low hanging cloud
dew around the house
how did a cloud get in the house
even if showing rage feels new
it is time to push our
    underestimated
            parts to
            perform
        calculating
        how many
        nails to
        overtake
        a hammer

my fingernails
growing faster
or I am losing
track of time
this is not the song kept holy
it is the one with all the faucets on
you have to or
someone has to
make its heart stop
before you eat it
please remember
the heart stopper must
do his job in time for supper
my choice to not cut my hair
until my nation's wars end
took the responsibility
of death by strands
heart stoppers all
our war against
all living beings
must end now
end now end
now end now
end now end
now end now

the reporter refers to the theater
as a cultural campus
                    a
                    tongue
                    to
                    corporate
                    fundamentals
                    of
                    pleasure
                    my boyfriend
                        calls to say
                        You Are My
                        Solar Plexus
                    language again
                    leaning against
                    a painting of an
                    ocean about to
                    be swallowed
                    by an ocean
                        I Love You
                        Too I say

no one needs to explain
we have reached a place
without comparison
there is no louder
siren than the one
outside the door
we are late
to need
no denying it
but are we ready for a
world without presidents
a day without Caligula swagger
are we ready to make a freak show of
our hearts say *yes* just say *yes*
God came down
to walk among
Herself *living*
imagined
beauty
begins
now
She
said

we mention the
cat aging in place
of the obvious but
it wasn't like that
we are not afraid
of growing old so
long as we know
love each day
what has happened to you
writing a poem about love
what has happened to any
of us for thinking we
can possibly
survive
even
reasonably
without
it
because
nothing
keeps
me wanting life like love

load your lips
with your song
argue for beauty
always argue for beauty
it is the one fight we are
forbidden to surrender
never let them believe
we know the way
out of its clutch
this above all
will help us
feel less
alone in the world
when approaching danger
we make note of when
our bravery runs out
and know the rest
of our struggle
is fueled
by Love
nothing
else it
could
be

this is not a writer's retreat
it is another opportunity
to throw the bridle off
accept a clock
made of flowers
hyacinth to lilac
lilac to lily of the valley
lily of the valley to rose
our olfactory
intoxication
timetable

whenever a
path is gone to seed
voices around me have more song
stitches of nutrients hold us together
bring us to life with a tolling bell
a solid infringement pressed
into the cold vanished calm
in the fur of this sentence
my animal psalm for you

RESURRECT EXTINCT VIBRATION:
A (Soma)tic Poetry Ritual

I
___

Amanda Paradise is the author of this book, and *by CAConrad* is its title. I did not mention this earlier because I did not want to interrupt your conversation with the poems. A (Soma)tic poetry ritual I did a few years previously to overcome my depression after my boyfriend Earth's rape and murder led me to "Resurrect." I was sitting on a forest floor in New Hampshire when I realized that this man I loved, who had changed his name to Earth, died from the very same wounds humans inflict on the planet: he was bound and gagged, beaten, tortured, raped, then covered in fossil fuels and set on fire. This connection brought a flood of grief. After my tears subsided, I lay flat on the fallen leaves, feeling my breath sync with the soil beneath me and with the wind, birds, insects—and as suddenly as I had burst into tears came a lavish shower of peace. It was extraordinary, instantly feeling these connections in my body. These sensations guided me to the "Resurrect."

At the time of finishing this book, I have been living on the road for 7 years. I drive back and forth across the United States to teach and to perform my poetry, and for the past 3 years, I did the "Resurrect" ritual in each state I was visiting. There are many ingredients to this ritual, which I will explain. Still, the main one involves lying on the ground with speakers playing field recordings of the many birds, mammals, insects, and reptiles now extinct or significantly depleted in numbers in my lifetime. The speakers are placed by my feet first, then are slowly moved up my body, my cells incorporating the sound waves. From the first time I did this, I was shocked that instead of feeling melancholy from hearing these recently extinguished fellow-creatures, I felt joy. I was elated, as if having a conversation with dear old friends. My guilt from these unexpected reactions braided themselves with my guilt of surviving many lovers and friends who died of AIDS.

One of my goals with "Resurrect" was to focus on an Ecopoetics beyond our degraded soil, air, and water, and to consider the concept of vibrational absence. The World Wildlife Association's biennial report revealed the most harrowing fact that more than 70 percent of our planet's wild creatures have disappeared in the past four decades. When a species becomes extinct, they take their sounds with them: breath, footfall, heartbeat, wing flutter, cry, and song. Their absent sounds change the collective frequency of the planet: a missing melody to melt the ice! In turn, we replace their sounds with our human din of metal, machines, bombs, drones, and cars. The altered pattern of our planet's assembled resonance is my focus. When I was born over half a century ago, my infant cells proliferated on a significantly higher wild organic vibration than the cells of children born today. "Resurrect" momentarily returns the music of the disappeared back to the air, the body, and the land.

2

Humans have used the hand ax for over a million years. Interestingly, the design changed very little, which is quite a tribute to its form's success and use. Homophobia—a *very nice* word for Heterosexual Violence—is so ingrained, so systemic, because of its usefulness; otherwise, we would have changed it long ago. Heterosexual Violence remains a convenient tactical method to instill fear of the human body. Most people have varying degrees of homosexual desires, and outlawing such tendencies is a perfect way to encourage everyone to police themselves and one another constantly. Those who rank *too queer* on the spectrum are targets for anyone who wishes to violate their true desires. Like other weapons of control, Heterosexual Violence gave us empires.

Monotheism's holy scriptures have wielded this violence against queers for centuries. I have friends who are Jewish, Christian, and Muslim, all beautiful, caring, nonjudgmental people, but where I grew up in rural America, the form of Christianity practiced is brutal and terrifying. The conflation of Heterosexual Violence and the wanton destruction of the planet is in this same harsh biblical interpretation. When I was a child in the 1970s, a group of people wanted to build a recycling center in the county. Everyone in my family and the town were angry at being told that what they did with their garbage was harming the planet. At church with my grandmother, I remember the pastor angrily quoting Genesis, stating that God gave us dominion over the earth and all the creatures on it. He referred to the people who proposed the recycling center as ungodly and Communist, and the refrain of his sermon was, "DON'T THEY KNOW JESUS IS COMING!?" His message was to live by the scripture to please God so we can be granted Heaven one day. What we do to the planet does not matter; getting to Heaven is the only meaningful goal. When I was later Outed in high school as queer, I finally fully understood just how brutal violence sanctioned by God can feel on the body and spirit. The ruling Christian patriarchy in America is a brand of sadism Europeans got rid of centuries ago.

Conversations about our planet's endangerment must occur. The practice of this work included making drawings of extinct animals on index cards and writing a short message about the creature along with an email contact. I then left these cards on buses and subways, in coffee shops, hotel lobbies, laundromats, libraries, and community centers across the nation. I replied to each inquiry as the animal, discussing the fragility of my habitat, my courtship habits, my taste in food, how I raise my children, and finally that I am dead and that my children are also dead—that in fact my species was recently wiped out. I also provided information on theories of how we became extinct, as found in reports by ornithologists, entomologists, mammalogists, marine biologists, and others who study the recent rise and fall of the many species of life on our planet.

I also filled the trunk of my car with plastic flowers and small white tags to tie near dead animal bodies along the highway. For instance: DEER / Hit And Run Victim On Route 36 / Missouri, September 2018 / Next Of Kin Unknown.

3

I became vegan and macrobiotic in 1988, when scores of friends were dying of AIDS, and I was always urging them to join me for the health benefits. I must admit that when I became vegan, it was not originally for animal rights. I now continue being vegan to be a better advocate for our fellow creatures, but as a child I hunted deer, rabbits, pheasants, and squirrels. I wanted this (Soma)tic poetry ritual based on extinct and endangered animals to include a meditation on the animals whose lives I took when I was a young hunter.

Whisper was the name of my hunting dog. After I received my first rifle at 9, she and I loved to explore the forest and meadows. When I shot a squirrel, she would retrieve it and hover eagerly, waiting for me to give her the heart as I skinned and cleaned the body in a stream, then secured it to sticks to roast over a fire. I now refer to Whisper as my Lord of the Flies companion, and she would be sad if she were alive today to find that I no longer kill and eat squirrels in the forest.

For this ritual ingredient, I drew a silhouette of Whisper with black ink. Then I made a kite out of sticks and paper, gluing Whisper's image to the front. I made secret notes on another piece of paper with words I used for her when hunting, then glued it to the back of the kite. When I sent it in the air, her rough portrait faced the sky above me, the wind pushing my secret messages into her shape on the other side. Because we lived in the country, she never knew the tug of a leash, so it felt odd having the kite pull against my wrist, but at the same time, I liked it, getting to feel the weight of the wind on her drawing. I took notes for the poem while flying my old friend above me.

In the evening, I cut her silhouette from the kite and placed it under my pillow. The dreams were beguiling: a realm of moss on tall trees, lily of the valley, and many shards of light dancing on everything. Whisper was not there as I knew her but some-how all around me. It was a place where I felt myself relax. Then I realized that I was resting in the dream where I had buried her when I was newly a teenager. I was visiting my old friend all along in luxuriant consolation! After waking, I took more notes for the poem.

There were many memories of my time with Whisper to sift through; for instance, whenever I gave her a squirrel heart while cleaning the flesh, she would run in circles around me, which widened as she ran faster and faster until she collapsed, exhausted. When I was a child, I thought she loved squirrel hearts, and that was that, but now I am not so sure. It was the only time she would run like that until exhausted. It was the heart muscle of this very anxious, speedy creature she had just eaten. Could it be she was taking on the squirrel's vibration, running with the creature's last memory of total panic and fear of being hunted?

4

For this ritual ingredient, I used two different crystals as mediums between plants. One was exclusively for indoor plants, another for wild plants.

Indoors: I placed the crystal for several hours on a potted plant's soil near the stem. Later, I held the crystal in my left hand while taking notes for the poem. Then I would whisper to the crystal to relay the plant's message to another plant, and I would place it in the next pot. When writing with the crystal in my hand, I could feel a calm conversation, concentrated on drifting through the seasons. Their vocabulary for moving through time is something I feel drawn to remember in my body while swinging my arms and walking with my reveries for this world's possibilities. I also watched Kenneth Anger's *Inauguration of the Pleasure Dome* with the indoor plants.

Outdoors: This crystal moved between wild plants, meaning only plants whose seeds were transported by birds, wind, or some other natural force. I placed the crystal near a plant for a few hours. Later, the guardedness I felt while writing with the crystal did not make sense until I realized that somebody had mowed the meadow a few feet away. How had I not discovered this straight off? There I was, the selfish human, not thinking that somebody had cut thousands of other plants to their knees, their bodies strewn everywhere, the pungent odor of chlorophyll pouring from their wounds in the hot sun.

In the past, I have used crystals to speak between trees and other plants and animals, but with this one, I found a new relationship to received languages for the poems. I can glean from them in these writing sessions; the plants tell me that their ability to change carbon dioxide into oxygen is also transforming the words I write. Maybe, a better word is *translate*, meaning the leaves are a kind of translation device. It feels like a sentence in the conversation comes back with one word changed, giving an entirely new interpretation to both the ritual and the resulting poem. The leaves tell me they are a mirror, but nothing like the kind we humans experience. While the outdoor, wild plant crystal had more life-threatening circumstances, there was beneath that a vibration similar to the indoor plant crystal's language for the movement of time, though more urgent, a pulsing pressure running through my body. I placed the crystal under my pillow so their song could enter my sleeping body of dreams, and I whispered, "Vegetables, sisters, brothers, unfurl a bit more with me in the poem."

5

When I lived in Philadelphia, I had a small plot in a community garden. It was a place to retrieve a bit of the magic of gardening I had enjoyed as a child growing up in the country. With an old Polaroid camera, I made a snapshot collection of my okra, beets, and string beans from their first signs of life, to their first leaves, and finally of their full abundance of vegetables.

There was a place online for members of the garden to write to other members. I disliked reading it because it became a dump for complaints and accusations: claims of someone's stealing tomatoes and other petty nonsense. When rumors began circulating that the city would sell the garden to a contractor who wanted to build a condominium, it was the beginning of the end. And it did happen. One day I arrived at the garden with my spade and plant food to find bulldozers destroying everything. That was years ago, the piles of fresh soil and worms for our garden plots long gone now.

For the "Resurrect" ritual, I took the photographs of my garden back to Philadelphia. At the condominium, I pushed a few of the doorbells until someone buzzed me in. I found my way into the basement, which had washing machines and storage lockers. I walked to the part of the building where my former garden plot used to exist. It was exciting being underground in the basement, and I lay on the concrete floor, looking up to the ceiling. Where there are now wires, pipes, and light fixtures, I imagined my vegetables' roots dangling above me. I brought fresh string beans, which I slowly chewed while looking at the photographs of my garden. The roots used to grip soil at this very spot, hello, *hello*, where are you now?

For several years I have been eating small amounts of different mushrooms for their various health benefits: Reishi, Shitake, Lion's Mane, Turkey Tail, Chaga, and others. They have helped me with inflammation, boosted my immune system, and provided other benefits. What we know about mushrooms and their feathery thread-like mycelium root systems, called hyphae, is that they have an ancient relationship with plants. This primordial, symbiotic connection is complex and involves, among other things, assisting the water and nutrient transport for plants. The daily mushroom consumption-saturation I have undergone these past few years has awakened my cells to the ongoing conversations between these two lifeforms. For the first time in my life, I can garner messages from plants—not words, but a frequency, introducing me to my very own grand and beautiful inner-cosmos.

In the basement, directly beneath where my garden used to be, I burned the photographs one at a time. I drew a spiral on the concrete floor with the ashes, took notes for my poem, then left the building and left the city.

6

I knew very little about factory farming's brutality until I became vegan, which was in the early years of AIDS. "Resurrect" is a (Soma)tic poetry ritual for making contact with extinct animals—of Necromancy. I also wanted contact with lovers and friends who died when we were young, people who had many conversations with me about animals' lives.

There are many dead people in my past, not all of whom died of AIDS, but a large number of these beautiful souls did. I searched for a way to contact them that was universal, and I do not mean through a kind of portal in the sense of organized religion, but something secular we had all shared or visited. There was no location I was sure everyone had seen, no restaurant or park or beach. Then I thought about how a movie could be considered a place. *The Wizard of Oz* was a film I knew for sure all of these friends had visited. I call this *The Wizard of Oz* Portal.

I have also been thinking a lot about the hypogeum in ancient Greece. Hypogea were circular burial chambers, and pregnant women would visit their dead ancestors' remains to invite them to inhabit the bodies of their unborn babies. I hope that in a past life I was a pregnant woman who performed this ritual. It sounds terrifying, seeing the bones of the dead. Still, it is exciting thinking of such an experience coursing through my electrical circuitry and nervous system, my blood pumping into the heart of my unborn child and my ancestor simultaneously.

Do you remember the film's scene where the wicked witch puts Dorothy into an opium-induced trance in the poppy field? It is an essential part of the story, because after Dorothy is pulled out of the trance, she can finally see the solutions for the way out of fear and suffering. And it is when she is asleep in the poppies that I freeze the frame, then sit across the room with binoculars, studying Dorothy while quietly invoking the names of dead lovers and friends.

One night I dreamed that I walked past a church from which singing poured onto the street. When I walked inside, everyone I knew who had died of AIDS was there. They were fantastic and laughing and happy to see me, and I was so glad to see them. There has never been a dream as good as that one for me. Even my next best dream was only half as overwhelming with beauty, hugging, and talking with these friends. If I could get pregnant, I would want to be in a hypogeum with these friends and lovers and invite them to revisit the physicality of Earth through the life of my baby. Without hesitation, I would do it and write poems with my baby, a true collaboration. I very much enjoyed writing with *The Wizard of Oz* Portal.

7

Spirit whispering

into top of
my head

(shape of the poem "Golden in the Morning Crane Our Necks")

When I began writing using (Soma)tic poetry rituals, poems became shapes. At first I tried to allow the poem to languish on the left margin, but I felt ill. Then I felt anxious while also feeling compelled to move the lines off of the left margin. The more I pushed the words into the page's interior, the better I felt.

Muses, ghosts, spirits: I have no doubt of their existence. On occasion, I have met people who say they do not believe, and I am okay with that. For those who do believe in spirits who guide us in our poems, let me share a couple of things. One morning as I was waking, a voice came to me from the dimension I was, upon waking, about to leave. The voice said, "You have too many straight lines in your human world. We want to show you the way out of the violence of the line." After that, I never again resisted shaping the poems, and I was eager to allow all the help they wanted to offer.

Another morning the voice said, "The shape of a poem is the space between us. The poems are the bridge we use to one another." Who are you? "Many," was the answer. Many? I began thinking of all the beautiful people I knew who died, not just grandparents, whom I also loved, but the many souls I knew who died of AIDS. Painters, singers, prostitutes, janitors, poets, the many who died were somehow pushing up to my ear, to my hair and face, singing a little song for me to translate. From 1975 to 2005, they allowed me to write most of my poems on the left margin. Since 2005 they have wanted me to explore the broader reasons I find sustenance and strength in the poem's work.

8

My first crystal has been with me for 36 years. It was a gift, a large and exquisite piece of amethyst from my dear friend Peppy, who died of AIDS a few years later. She was a transwoman many of us young queers went to for comfort and guidance, our New Age Queen. She taught me to read tarot. She also requested that I create a ritual by which to masturbate her penis one last time before what we now call *Gender Confirmation Surgery*. She not only introduced me to the amethyst, she taught me how to live with it, and how to breathe and heal with it. We had many sick lovers and friends dying around us at the time, and the things she taught me are as vital today as they were when I first worked with her as a teenager.

I dedicate this ritual ingredient of "Resurrect" to Peppy. I took 4 solid copper water bottles and placed 9 crystals in each: 3 of amethyst, 3 of carnelian, and 3 rose quartz. Each container was then filled with water and sealed. I buried one in Minneapolis, one in Memphis, and one in Cheyenne, forming a triangle. The fourth was buried in Omaha, situated in the center of the triangle, and I called it The Seat Of The Crystal Grid.

In Omaha, I buried the container in a secluded edge of a field just outside the city. I would get naked and sit with the crystal-filled copper container directly beneath me, and with a compass, I would align myself with Minneapolis. I then ate small amounts of dirt from the Minneapolis site and listened to an ambient recording I made at the location. Once I felt attuned, I flooded my body with the recordings of recently extinct animals while writing. Then I would turn clockwise toward Memphis, eat a little dirt from the Memphis location, and listen to the site's ambient recording. After writing, I would shift position facing Cheyenne to repeat the process of dirt and recordings and writing. In the fall of 2019, I dug up the containers, brought them to Philadelphia, and left the crystals on the doorstep to Peppy's old building. My love to you, dear friend, teacher, sister, until we meet again in the next life.

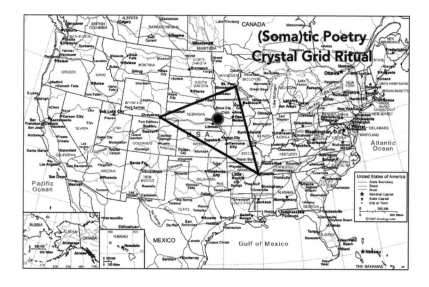

9

Walmart is a chain of retail stores with over 9,000 locations in the lower 48 states. They are massive: the average store sells hundreds of thousands of items, and the larger stores can hold more than half a million products. Sleeping in your vehicle overnight is permitted at most locations, and as a result, there is often a handful of giant, expensive travel vans parked together. There are also poor people living in cars, sometimes entire families.

When I woke in the morning, I would study the terrain surrounding the store with binoculars. If I were in Florida, I saw palm trees; if I were in Arizona, there was desert, or in Montana, mountains towered in the background. No matter where I was, once I entered the store, it became a portal into The Walmart Dimension, with the same "greeter" at the entrance, the same music playing, same items for sale. I would listen to a recording of extinct animals and walk in a giant spiral formation, kneeling in the store's center to take notes for the poems.

I always follow these rules for sleeping in a car: (1) Always sleep in the driver's seat. (2) Always keep doors locked. (3) Always keep windows closed no matter how hot it is. (4) Always keep the key in the ignition. (5) Always park so that the car has a clean shot ahead.

There were several close calls. In West Virginia, I had a gun pulled on me, and another time someone cut my tires. In Alabama, I woke to half a dozen young men near the car; one of them bent to look in the driver's side window. He yelled, "It's a *dude*, not a chick!" Another yelled, "A *faggot*!" One of them approached the car with a baseball bat, and I lurched forward, turned the key, and floored the gas. In the rearview mirror I saw them run to their vehicles to pursue me. Once I got on the highway, I kept a steady speed while my adrenaline pumped. Rule 6: Always have a full tank of gas.

I pulled myself off the road when the COVID-19 pandemic struck in 2020. (Soma)tic poetry rituals are prepared for the unexpected. I brought the "Resurrect" ritual inside with me. For several months I stayed with my old friend Elizabeth Kirwin; this was our second plague, as we had many friends die of AIDS when we were much younger and living in Philadelphia. For decades friends and lovers have given me crystals as gifts, some crystals passed forward from those who died. I arranged the crystals into a triangle, with a giant copper lightning rod coated in gold in the center, conducting the crystals' energy to its point. The golden rod was a gift from the artist Jason Dodge. I looped a thin copper wire around my neck, and the other end around the tip of the golden rod, and would meditate for 36 minutes, then write. Several nights after these intense sessions with the crystal grid, I experienced astral projection. One night, floating above the house, I wondered if we can succumb to viruses in the astral body.

Most of the poems in this book came from giant blocks of notes that I would chip away at and arrange into poems. The writing I did indoors with the crystals was different, these poems came out whole, often with no editing necessary, and they compose the long piece in the book, titled "72 Corona Transmutations." Thank you so much for reading.

ACKNOWLEDGMENTS

My thanks to everyone at Wave Books for taking such fantastic care with my poems.

My thanks to everyone at Creative Capital for their generous grant money and support.

My thanks to everyone at Headlands Center for the Arts in California where some of these pages were written.

My thanks to SPACE and Pickwick Independent Press in Portland, Maine.

My thanks to Porto Design Biennale 2021 for publishing me on Yūgen App.

My thanks to all of my amazing friends, whose love makes my poetry possible.

My thanks to the editors, publishers, translators, and designers who generously published these poems in their magazines, chapbooks, and broadsides.

MAGAZINES

Arc Poetry Magazine, The Babel Tower Notice Board, BEAST, The Believer, Blazing Stadium, blush, Bodega, Boog City, Carrier Pigeon, Catamaran, Cultured, Cunning Folk, The Dalhousie Review, F A N - T A S M A, F(r)iction, Hurricane Review, Interim, Jewish Currents, jubilat, Lambda Literary Review, Lit Hub, LiVE MAG!, Neon Pajamas, Peripheries, Pet Fish, Pfeil Magazine, POESIA, Poetry, Poetry Wales, The River Rail, The Scores, Silver Pinion, and *Sublevel*

ANTHOLOGIES

Athens Art Biennale catalogue, edited by Christoforos Marinos (2020)

Baltic Art Triennial 13 catalogue, edited by Cédric Fauq (2019)

The Beautiful, edited by Dana Teen Lomax (Black Radish Books, 2019)

The Body In Language, edited by Edwin Torres (Counterpath Press, 2019)

Dead of Winter, edited by Kim Jacobs-Beck, Miranda Scharf, and Jasmine Warner (Milk & Cake Press, 2021)

Everyone is an Artist: Cosmopolitical Exercises with Joseph Beuys at the Kunstsammlung Nordrhein-Westfalen in Düsseldorf, edited by Eugen Blume, Susanne Gaensheimer, Isabelle Malz, and Catherine Nichols (Hatje Cantz Verlag, 2021)

The Experiment Will Not Be Bound (Unbound Edition Press, 2021)

Intertitles, edited by Jess Chandler, Aimee Selby, Hana Noorali, and Lynton Talbot (Prototype, 2021)

Queer Nature: An Ecoqueer Poetry Anthology, edited by Michael Walsh (Autumn House Press, 2021)

Ramifications, edited by Sam Buchan-Watts (Clinic Presents, 2021)

Rewilding: An Ecopoetic Anthology (Crested Tit Collective, 2020)

Spells: 21st-Century Occult Poetry, edited by Sarah Shin and Rebecca Tamás (Ignota Books, 2019)

Urban Ecology, edited by Christina Irmen (University of Pennsylvania Press, 2020)

Watch Your Head, edited by Sina Queyras et al. (Coach House Books, 2020)

We Want It All: An Anthology of Radical Trans Poetics, edited by Andrea Abi-Karam and Kay Gabriel (Nightboat Books, 2020)

CHAPBOOKS

18 Corona Transmutations (Golden Boomerang Press, 2021)

18 Poems & (Soma)tic Rituals (Hallie Ford School of Graduate Studies Press/PNCA, 2019)

Bathe the Door with Blood of the Centaur (Catalpa, 2020)

Seized by the Left Hand (Dundee Contemporary Arts, 2020)

Archivorum Advent Calendar: Sustainability Edition

"Glitter in My Wounds" broadside by Umang Antariksh Sagar

"low hanging cloud" broadside by Brandon Menke

"Memories of Why I Stopped Being a Man" broadside by Radical Paper Press

Art News (translated into Lithuanian by Monika Kalinauskaite)

God Is the Space between Us (translated into Spanish by Cristine Brache for Anonymous Gallery)

Queer Poets in Greek (translated into Greek by Sam Albatros)

and suddenly it all blossoms, exhibition at Riga International Biennial of Contemporary Art (Jelgavas Tipogrāfija, Riga, 2021)

Are You Ready?, television show by Gitte Sætre and Frans Jacobi (Norway, 2021)

Auguries Cast Aside, show by Jason Dodge (Karma Gallery, NYC, 2019)

BOY BOX, show by Angela Conant (EFA Project Space and PPOW Gallery, NYC, 2021)

Don't Touch Me: Acts of Faith, show by Precious Okoyomon (Robert Grunenberg Gallery, Berlin, 2019)

"Freeflow," published two recordings of poems (NTS x Montblanc, UK, 2020)

It's Time All the Time for Radical Friendship, exhibition by Alex Alonso (Futura, Prague, 2020)